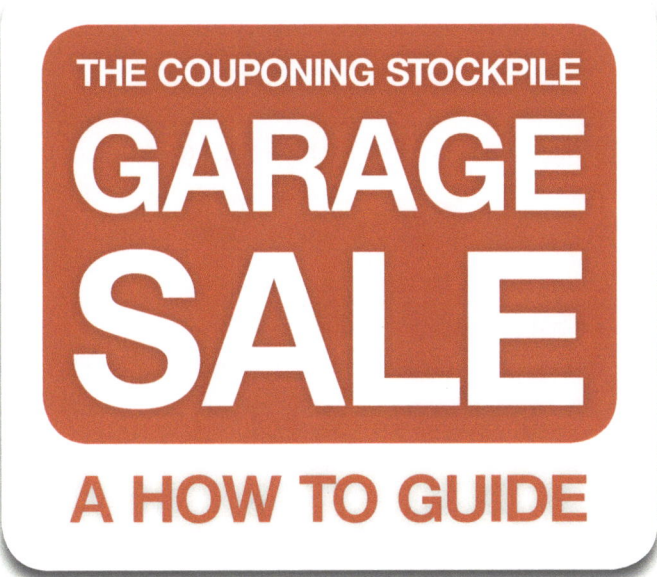

Jenny Dean

Disclaimer

The information contained in this guide is for informational purposes only.

I am a couponer and a garage sale queen. Any advice that I give is my opinion based on my own experiences. You should always ask your city about garage sale ordinances in your neighborhood. You also need to use your own common sense when it comes to executing these strategies in your neck of the woods.

Please understand that there are unique links contained in the *The Couponing Stockpile Garage Sale: A How To Guide*, and if you click on that link on a particular day and purchase something during that Amazon session, I may receive a variable commission primarily based upon the sales price and item purchased. While that doesn't increase the cost to you, I do get a referral fee as a commission.

The material in this guide may include information, products or services by third parties. Third Party Materials are comprised of the products and opinions expressed by their owners. As such, I do not assume responsibility or liability for any Third Party material or opinions.

The publication of such Third Party Materials does not constitute my guarantee of any information, instruction, opinion, products or services contained within the Third Party Material. The use of recommended Third Party Materials does not guarantee any success and/or earnings related to you. Publication of such Third Party Material is simply a recommendation and an expression of my own opinion of that material.

No part of this publication shall be reproduced, transmitted, or sold in whole or in part in any form, without the prior written consent of the author. All trademarks and registered trademarks appearing in this guide are the property of their respective owners.

Users of this guide are advised to do their own due diligence when it comes to making decisions about garage sales and the like and all information, products, services that have been provided should be independently verified by you. By reading this guide, you agree that I and my website, GuideToCouponing.com, are not responsible for the success or failure of your couponing stockpile garage sale decisions relating to any information presented in this *The Couponing Stockpile Garage Sale: A How To Guide*

©2013 Jenny Dean GuideToCouponing.com. All Rights Reserved

Table of Contents

Disclaimer	2
Introduction	5
Organize Your Stuff	8
How to Price Your Items	12
Layout - How to Lay Out Your Garage Sale	15
Timing - When to Have the Garage Sale	17
Advertise – Let Your Sale Be Known!	19
Before First Days of Sale	21
Before, after and During the Sale	32
Have Fun	36
Safety and Legal	37
Future Sales	38
Online Resources	39
Garage Sale Sign Checklist	40
Things to Do 3-4 Days before the Sale	41
Things to Do the Day of the Sale	42
Things to Do after the Sale	43
Garage Sale Checklist	44

The Couponing Stockpile Garage Sale: A How To Guide is the second in a series of books that I will be releasing on GuideToCouponing.com. For over seven years I have not only studied, but read, heard and experienced how to coupon legally and effectively and then have garage sales to sell coupon stockpiles.

Much of what I experienced hosting couponing stockpile garage sales is what I will talk about in this book – I will teach you garage sale basics and more importantly, how to have a successful sale and how to continue to have more successful sales. In many ways it was difficult to keep this book relatively short. However, I wanted to stick to the main point of *How To*.

Even if you don't have a coupon stockpile, this book is packed full of ideas, tips and tricks so that you can have a successful garage sale.

Please enjoy this book and let me know if there are items you disagree with or if there are subjects you think I could expand on or make improvements on.

I do ask that you please keep this book to yourself. I have spent years not only researching and gathering information but actually writing the book as well. My interest in selling this book is so that I can dedicate more of my time researching ways to make the most of our couponing habits!

New to couponing? You might want to first read our *Couponing for the Beginner: A Guide to Couponing for the Uninitiated*.

If you haven't already, I encourage you to subscribe to GuideToCouponing.com's newsletter, join us on Facebook, Pinterest, Twitter, Google+ and YouTube!

Introduction

I come from a long line of Garage Sale women – my mom and my aunt have an annual garage sale and I have two of my own per year (there are ordinances in my city that say I can only have two sales a year and I think I would limit it to that too because I don't think my neighbors are keen on me having a lot of garage sales).

I am also a crazy couponer (I sell my couponing stock pile twice a year) and have not only been asked how I get all my stuff for free or for next to nothing, but also how I have successful garage sales. Friends usually say, "Oh, I tried to have a garage sale once – total flop." Well, it doesn't have to be – your efforts can be fruitful!

The thing is - mine are never a flop. Sure some are better than others. Garage sales can be unpredictable, but you can take measures to make them more predictable.

This book will teach you why my yard sales are not a total flop. It took years of practice – not only couponing for years, but years of doing garage sales to learn how to do them right.

I make anywhere from $600-$2000 per garage sale and over the course of two to three days that can be a pretty nice amount.

Even if you're not a crazy couponer looking to sell your stockpile, but are looking to have a garage sale, you will benefit from the tips in this book.

Thanks to TLC's Extreme Couponing show having a stockpile garage sale is now easier than ever. How so? Well, before the show was created – I was asked a number of questions by garage sale attendees:

The Couponing Stockpile Garage Sale: A How To Guide

- "Did you rob a pharmacy?"
- "Are you a rep or something?"
- "Did you close your store?"

Now, those questions are few and far between - most garage sale go-ers have now been to a stockpile sale and get excited about them. In fact, now I get comments like:

- "Oh! I love these kinds of sales!"
- "Oh! I wish I could learn to coupon like this!"
- "Oh I get it...are you an extreme couponer?"

If you have read Couponing for the Beginner and have started executing some of the couponing tips and tricks therein then you might now have a stockpile and need to get rid of product for a profit. Sure you could donate it - but you might be like me and prefer to sell it for a profit.

I started to have garage sales to help make ends meet and to pay for many things - like having the house painted, paying for groceries and more. I not only have two garage sales a year, but I also sell a lot of my stockpile on Craig's List or through people I met through Craig's List or through the Garage Sales - more to come on that later. I also sell on Amazon.com and eBay.

Please enjoy this book and let me know if there are things you disagree with or if there are subjects you think I could expand or improve upon.

I do ask that you please keep this book to yourself. I have spent years not only researching and gathering information but actually writing the book as well. My interest in selling this book is so that I can dedicate more of my time researching better deals and ways to save you more money as well.

If you haven't already, I encourage you to subscribe to GuideToCouponing.com's newsletter.

The purpose of *The Couponing Stockpile Garage Sale: A How To Guide* is to teach you HOW TO have a successful garage sale by selling your couponing stockpile. You'll learn how to organize your stuff, how to price things, what to price your items, how to advertise, how to make garage sale signs and much more.

Here's to the garage sale god(dess) in you!

Organize Your Stuff

If you're having a stock pile sale then you want to organize your stuff – unless you already have it super-organized like many of the couponers featured on Extreme Couponing, for example.

Hey, it's a garage sale, after all, so I also throw in some "regular" garage sale items – like clothes, odds and ends, etc. to sell with my stockpile. If you have a chair, a couch, a table – anything big to put towards the end of the driveway to get people to stop, that's the best thing – and you want your garage sale to look like you have a lot of stuff - AT ALL TIMES.

TABLES

One of the most important things is to have tables - lots of folding tables so that you can collapse them and put them away every day easily. These tables are sold at places like Target and Walmart - but again, the idea is to make money at a garage sale, not spend it. So, you can always see if you can borrow tables from friends, family, your kid's school, your church, etc. The table pictured here is the kind to shoot for.

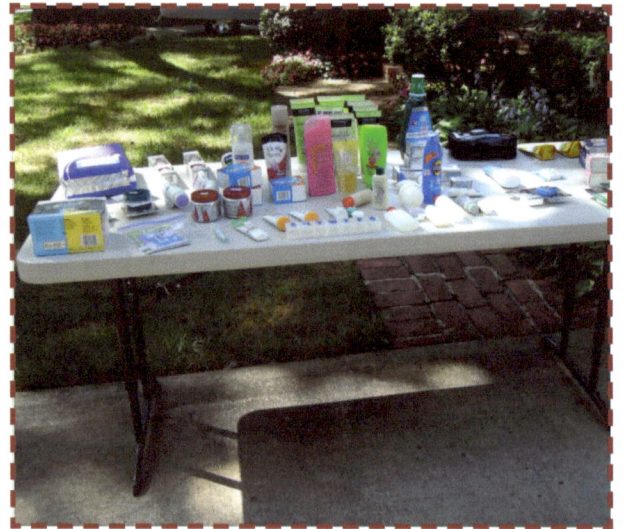

GuideToCouponing.Com

If you don't have access to these collapsible tables, you can use saw horses and lay something flat on top of them – doors, plywood, etc. Don't have saw horses? You could use chairs. Also, picnic tables are great – you can use the top of the table and the seats. Card tables, coffee tables, the kitchen tables! If you place clothing or stuffed animals or other things on the ground, use a tarp or a blanket so things aren't directly on the ground. And they look more inviting. A lot of couponers have success using table cloths to cover their tables – but that's a little too much in my opinion. It's your call on that one!

If you have a chain link fence - they make a great place to hang clothing. You can also use a wooden clothes dryer to display items.

I talk more about tables and signs in this video on YouTube. (http://youtu.be/YbLxARRrz5A)

SIGNS. SIGNS, SIGNS

Did I say signs? You bet I did. CLEAR SIGNS.

Be sure to have excellent signage – as with any product, if you are not known, you are not found! Be sure you are known, so people can find you and **BUY**!

You not only need signs on the streets near and around your home so that people can find your home and your sale, but you also want signs for bulk items. First, let's cover street signs.

I like to find event signs or political signs that are expired. When the event is over or when the political election is over, I pull them from their spot - and then take off the cardstock portion and turn it inside out to reveal the all-white inside. I then print "Garage Sale" "MY ADDRESS" and a huge arrow in HUGE letters. I think use packing tape (that, of course, I got for free at CVS) and tape everything to the sign.

The Couponing Stockpile Garage Sale: A How To Guide

Here is a YouTube video that explains how I go about making signs and I like to have 8-10 of these signs. Garage Sale Sign - How to Make a Homemade Garage Sale Sign - Guide to Couponing (http://youtu.be/i2YabxYKiL0)

Be sure to check whether there are restrictions on placements of signs in your neighborhood and whether you need a permit to hold a garage sale.

SIGNS FOR BULK ITEMS

Let's say you have a ton of some item. Whether it be 2 liter bottles of Pepsi or 50 Dawn dishwashing liquids – you can make a bulk sign and put it in front of those items. Or you can make a sign with a photo of the item on it plus the price of it to attract interest. My aunt started doing this with water years ago and we made a profit from selling bottled water while people shopped. I have done this with Coke too.

You also want "Cash Only" signs – sometimes I accept checks from regulars, but in general I would suggest that you take cash only. Makes life easier – and you don't have to worry about fees if the person has overdrawn their checking account. I have been asked if I took credit cards – I don't – but I have considered letting someone pay me with PayPal while they are standing there

checking out, if they need to. I would just wait until the payment came through on my phone to let them leave though!

You might even need "Not for Sale" signs – for example, sometimes the garage sale is also actually in my garage

10

and not just in my driveway. When that happens, I put "Not for Sale" signs on my shovels, rakes, etc. so that people stop asking me if they are for sale.

BOXES

Produce boxes like those found at Costco Warehouse for free – makes it very easy to transport it in and out of your garage. Citrus boxes are best, Avocadoes – they're made for a lot heavier weight, so they're heftier and will support more. Or you can use the crates as you see here – but you don't want to spend money http://youtu.be/YbLxARRrz5A - the idea is to make money. So if you can get boxes for free from Costco, all the better.

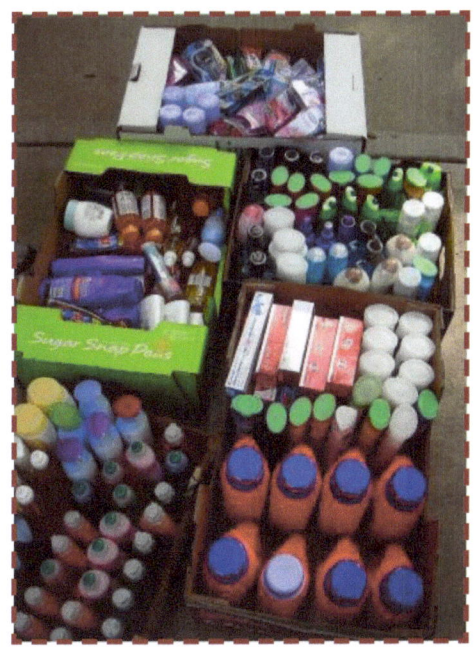

GROUPINGS

Group similar things together in those boxes, so that when you take them out on the driveway to unload them onto the tables, they are already organized as to where they need to go.

How to Price Your Items

There is somewhat of a debate as to how to price your items.

I have found that if I price them for half of what I "bought" them for - that seems to work well. For example, if I "bought" a Shampoo for $4 on sale, then I will mark it for $2.

That will usually make people think it's pretty cheap and a great price because they are used to paying $4. Also, if I bought (again, think of "bought" in quotes when I use that because, of course, I got them for free after coupons, rebates, etc.) for $4 on sale at CVS, then it's probably $3.50 or less at Wal-mart regularly, so $2 is still cheaper than Wal-mart.

I also use even numbers or numbers of our currency. For example, I price things at 25 cents, 50 cents, 75 cents, $1, $2, $3, $5, $10, $20. That way the amounts are whole amounts or when they add up they make whole amounts that people tend to carry on them.

SPREADSHEETS

You can certainly buy those little dot stickers and write your prices on them, or you can get garage sale stickers at OfficeMax, OfficeDepot or online that are already marked. Like these Avery Preprinted Removable Garage Sale Labels, 0.75 Inches, Round, Pack of 350.

Or you can do what I do – I have an Excel spreadsheet with prices on it. Like this:

	A	B	C	D	E	F	G	H	I
4	$1	$2	$1	$2	$10	$1	$2	$5	$1
5	$1	$2	$1	$2	$10	$1	$2	$5	$1
6	$1	$2	$1	$2	$10	$1	$2	$5	$1
7	$1	$2	$1	$2	$10	$1	$2	$5	$1
8	$1	$2	$1	$2	$10	$1	$2	$5	$1
9	$1	$2	$1	$2	$10	$1	$2	$5	$1
10	$1	$2	$1	$2	$10	$1	$2	$5	$1
11	$1	$2	$1	$2	$10	$1	$2	$5	$1
12	$1	$2	$1	$2	$10	$1	$2	$5	$1
13	$1	$2	$1	$2	$10	$1	$2	$5	$1
14	$1	$2	$1	$2	$10	$1	$2	$5	$1
15	$1	$2	$1	$2	$10	$1	$2	$5	$1
16	$1	$2	$1	$2	$10	$1	$2	$5	$1
17	$1	$2	$1	$2	$10	$1	$2	$5	$1

I then print it off on a pink piece of paper. I then cut out the individual prices and put them all in a Ziploc baggie with tape. When it comes time to price everything, I just pull out the bag, grab the price I need and then stick it on the product with a piece of adhesive tape like Scotch Magic Tape.

If you are having a sale with a lot of people (like five families) then you can color code your sale to keep track of each person's sales. For example:

- Jenny = PINK
- Jill = BLUE
- Jean = YELLOW

The Couponing Stockpile Garage Sale: A How To Guide

And when someone comes up with several items from all of you – you can add all the blue ones, mark that down for Jill. Add all the yellow and mark that down for Jean and then all the pink and mark that down for Jenny.

Another way to price your items is to have everything color coded - something along these lines:

- RED = $0.50
- YELLOW = $0.75
- BLUE = $1
- GREEN = $2
- PINK = $3
- WHITE = $5

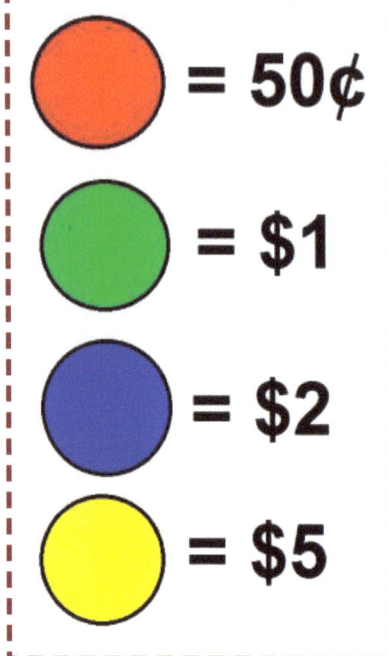

So in other words, all you have to do is grab those color-coded circle stickers from OfficeMax/Office Depot and then price things that way. Then when you have the sale, you can make signs on your computer. And then when you have the sale - you can tape the signs to the tables so people know how much things cost. You can also put one of the signs near the checkout table.

I have heard that other couponers will go so far as to cut out the sale prices from the store weekly flyers and then put those on cardboard next to the items to show them the real savings. Honestly, I find the idea of that terribly time consuming. The cost/benefit ratio on that one just doesn't work out for me.

I talk more about pricing items in this YouTube video http://youtu.be/9IVuoxZm5ys.

TRIAL SIZE ITEMS

I like to put them in little groups and then put them in Ziploc baggies and put a sticker on the outside. However, you can also always put them in a container and then make a sign that all trial sized items are $1 or whatever you want to charge.

Layout - How to Lay Out Your Garage Sale

As with any business (this is a business since you are selling and wanting to make a profit), you want to have a plan – not only in your execution, but also in your layout. Here is how I layout my garage sales.

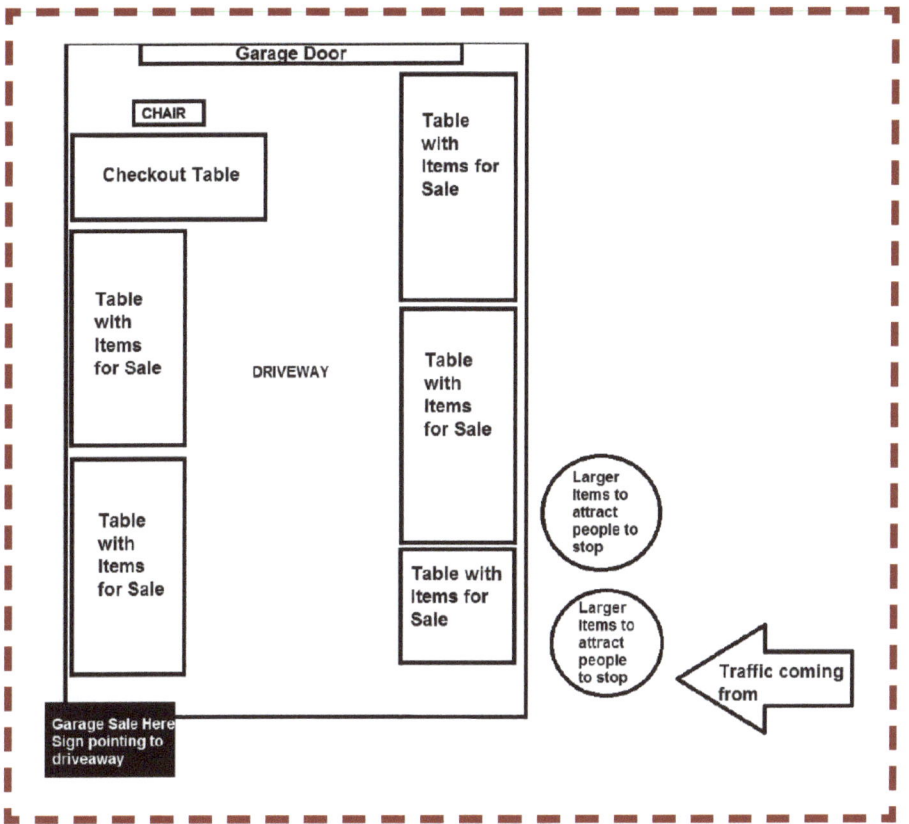

You'll notice that everything is out on my driveway – I don't actually have items for sale in my garage (I might do that if my garage was bigger, but it's only a 1-car garage and there's hardly room in there for a bunch of people to be shopping. I also like that they are further away from the door into my house. The checkout table is closest to the door into my house. You'll notice that I like to place big "attention grabber" items at the end of the driveway where the majority of the traffic comes from. I also like to add an additional "Garage Sale Here" sign at the end of the driveway with an arrow pointing in – there are many houses on my block and it helps people not to have to double guess.

When it comes to the tables - don't be afraid to move things around - when stuff is selling, bring out more stuff and fill the tables - always make the tables look full. For some reason garage salers (people that shop at garage sales) don't like when they haven't made it to the first day of the sale - they usually think they are getting leftovers or something. This, of course, isn't the case, but you've got to be aware of how people think – so be sure the tables always look full. If you start running low, then just collapse one of the tables and double the stuff up on another table.

Timing - When to Have the Garage Sale

When to have your garage sale has a lot to do with your schedule and what will work for you. Here are things to consider when scheduling a time to have your garage sale:

- **Good weather** – you want to have your garage sale when the weather is nice – not only because you'll be outside the entire day manning the thing, but also you want your shoppers to be comfortable while shopping. I've had them when it's too cold and people don't want to stay long because they are so cold. If you are limited on time and can't go with the flow – pick 2-3 weekends of potential garage sales and then as it gets closer and you're watching the weather go with the one that works out well. After reading some articles online, I found that June – October are the most popular months across the country in which to have a garage sale. That is usually when I have mine – although I did have a sale at the beginning of November this year because it was a super pleasant 60 degrees one weekend.

- **Days of the week** – you might want to experiment. It depends on the part of the country you're in and also where you live in your city. For example, I find that my sales do the best from Thursday – Saturday. But my mom and Aunt have had their sales start on a Wednesday and have found Wednesdays can be very profitable. This is where you live comes into play too – if you live in the 'burbs then you might want to do the weekend – but if you live in the city proper, you might get more traffic from people working at their jobs who want something to do on their lunch break.

- **Events –** is there some major event that happens in your city that brings a lot of traffic by your home? That's a good time to have a sale because there is more traffic and if your signs are right, the people will come!

- **Annual neighborhood garage sales –** many neighborhoods across the USA have annual neighborhood garage sales where the entire neighborhood is invited to hold a garage sale on the same weekend. These can be great because people like that they can "shop" at many houses at one time rather than just one. And of course, for the seller (You!) it's better because it brings more traffic. However, I have found in my neighborhood that I do better when I am the only one having it. The reason is because I live in a neighborhood built in the late 30s/early 40s and the traffic can be too much if many people are having garage sales.

- **Estate Sales –** is there a major estate sale that is happening near your home soon? I have found that people usually look up several sales in the same area, so that they can keep bargain shopping – this is the same idea of a neighborhood garage sale.

- **City Ordinances -** Check with your city to see if there are limitations to when you can and can't have your sale.

As they say, timing is everything and that goes for garage sales too. You really have to think like a marketer to get the most bang out of your buck during your garage sale and having it during another key event or on a beautiful weekend, always helps with the sales!

Advertise – Let Your Sale Be Known!

There are a lot of ways to advertise for free – like through Facebook and Craig's List. You can also advertise in the paper, that's your call based on your community and your budget. My budget is always $0, so the paper is a no-go. My Aunt and my mom stopped advertising in the paper years ago – they always ask people who come to the sale how they found out about it and the top answers are: email list (we'll cover this one later), signs or Craig's List.

There are many ways to advertise about your sale:

- Facebook
- Craig's List
- Your Local Newspapers
- Flyers
- Signs

Place free ads:

- Craig's List

I have never used these sites, but discovered it when researching for this book. They are also sites where you can list your garage sale that's happening!

- garagesalehunter.com
- yardsalesearch.com
- mytagsale.com

So we already covered the importance of signs, now for Craig's List.

Many people look for ads on Craig's List for Garage Sales. It is very important to include big item specific names in that listing so that searchers on Craig's List can find you!

Details of how to post and what to put in your posting are covered in the next chapter.

FLYERS

Post flyers at gathering places around town (the supermarket bulletin board is a good place to start). Your flyers should list the best offerings, including any recognizable brand names (Ethan Allen, Crate & Barrel, Frigidaire, etc.), and details of the sale. Head flyers with classic attention-getters, such as cleaning out the attic, 1,000s of items, moving after 30 years, and first-time tag sale. Save any lengthy descriptions for the flyers placed where readers can pause to peruse them.

- Church
- School

Advertise in your daily newspaper (your ad should run on a Friday for a Saturday sale), as well as in a weekly newspaper or two in your area. If the paper has a special tag-sale section that readers can cut out, make sure you're in it.

Before First Days of Sale

In addition to organizing there are some things you want to do before the first day of the sale:

ADVERTISE

First list your garage sale on Craig's List

POST AN AD ON CRAIG'S LIST

Your Craig's List Ad is very important.

Craig's List has a special area where you can list your ad.

1. First, go to Craig's List (http://craigslist.org)
2. Scroll until you find your state and then select your city (or one closest to you)
3. Then click on "post to classifieds"
4. Then click the radio button for "for sale"
5. Then scroll until you find "garage & moving sales"
6. The move forward with the posting

You need to include:

- Days, date and times of sale
- Your address, city, state and zip

The Couponing Stockpile Garage Sale: A How To Guide

- Detailed list of items you'll have including brand names
- Photos of your stuff or big items or groupings of items that you're selling.

The title of your ad on Craig's List should have both the words, "Garage Sale" and "Yard Sale" or whatever people call such sales in your neck of the woods – I have also heard, "tag sale" or "rummage sale" in some places.

Here are examples of ads:

Posting Title: Coupon Queen Garage Sale Stock Pile in Fairway!

You'll see how I tell them the kind of sale I am having and then I also include the area of town I live in.

Posting Description:

Coupon Queen – Coupon Diva Selling Stock Pile!

1,000s of items (see a quick list below) - Boxes available-you'll need them!

Thursday, Friday, Saturday and Sunday starting at 9am

ADDRESS

CITY, STATE

Brand new toiletry items - toothpaste, mouth wash, wet wipes, dish washing liquid, shampoo, body wash, tampons, pads, razors, hair dye, glade candles, tide detergent, body lotion, air wick freshmatic

School Supplies - pads of paper, pencil boxes, brand new pens, rulers, highlighters, folders, compasses

..and much much more!

1,000s of items (see a quick list below) - Boxes available because you'll need them!

Brand New Products at half their retail prices

Be sure to include some photos of your stuff – I use old photos from previous garage sales, but you could also always just take photos of your stuff in boxes (much like the Facebook example later on in this chapter).

And here's what it looks like to the visitor on Craig's List:

CL > kansas city > for sale / wanted > garage & moving sales
Reply to: your anonymous craigslist address will appear here Posted: 2013-04-25, 11:09AM CDT

Coupon Queen Garage Sale in Fairway (Your Area of Town)

1,000s of items (see a quick list below) - Boxes available-you'll need them!

Thursday, Friday, Saturday and Sunday starting at 9am

ADDRESS
CITY, STATE, ZIP

Brand New Products at half their retail prices:
Advil
Excedrin
Deodorants
Shampoos and conditioners
Air Fresheners
Quattro razors
Disposable razors
Nail Polish
Toothpaste -- Crest, Colgate, Aquafresh
Mouthwash
Allergy Medicine
Huggies wipes
Make-Up
Lotion
Body Wash
Cereal
Drinks
Stockings

The Couponing Stockpile Garage Sale: A How To Guide

I try to list as many things as we have as possible, because you never know what people might be searching for on Craig's List.

Snap a shot of your goodies and upload the photos with the message.

SEND OUT AN EMAIL

Of course, for your first stockpile garage sale, you might not have a solid email list, but if for some reason you do or if you just want to send one out to family and friends this is what you need to include:

SUBJECT: The Twins' Huge Garage Sale! Starts Thursday!

You'll notice that I use "The Twins" – this helps people remember which garage sale it is. My mom and aunt are identical twins and people always remember their sale because of it.

Body of Email:

The Twins' Huge Garage Sale!

Thursday, Friday, Saturday and Sunday (May 6-9) starting at 9am

YOUR ADDRESS

CITY, STATE & ZIP

Here are the details: http://kansascity.craigslist.org/gms/1721269289.html

Jewelry for Sale: http://kansascity.craigslist.org/jwl/1721279622.html

E-mail with questions.

Thanks, Jenny

You'll notice I don't give them my phone number. You can, of course, but honestly, I never have time to take calls on top of everything else going on.

GuideToCouponing.Com

FACEBOOK

Here is an example of what you can post:

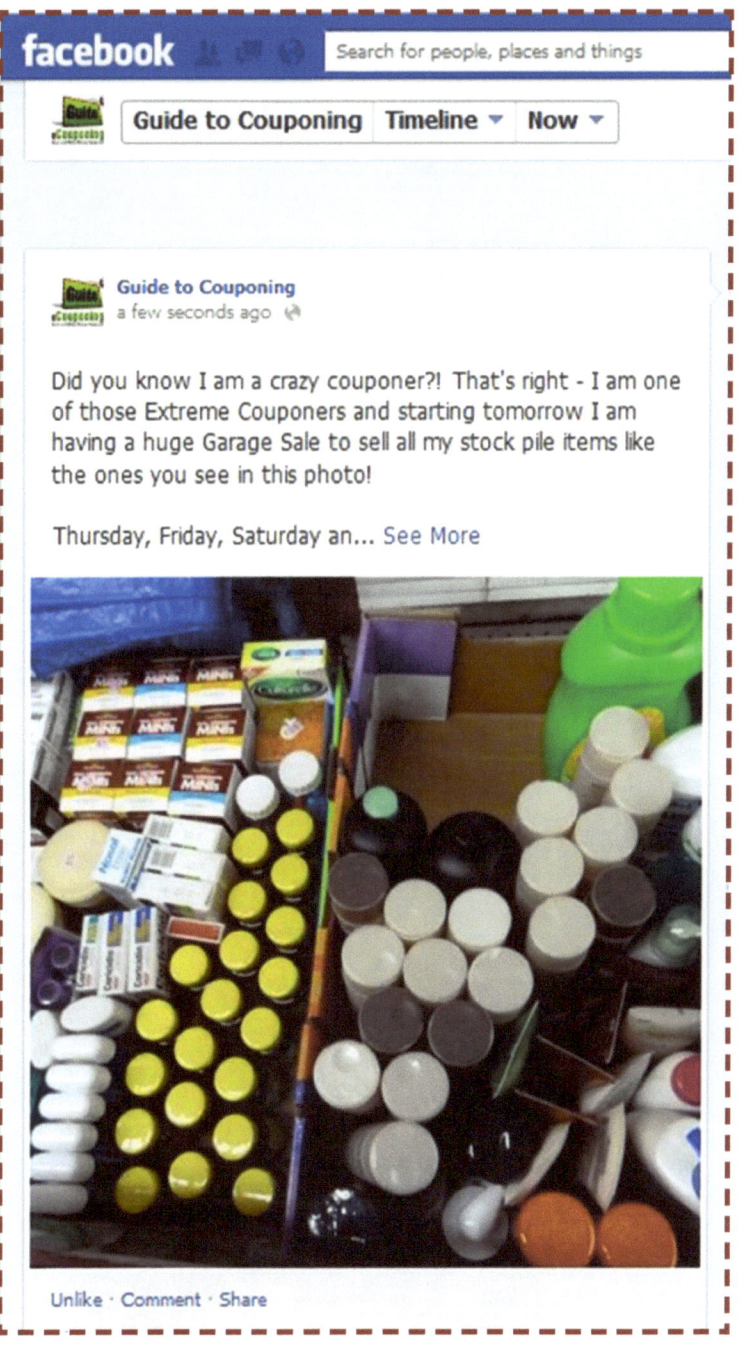

The Couponing Stockpile Garage Sale: A How To Guide

You'll notice that the photo is interesting enough that people take a second glance. And then you can tell that the "See More" allows you to expand to read the rest of it.

So then here's the rest of the message:

You'll see that you want to list:

- Your address
- Days of the sale and time of sale
- A link to your listing on Craig's List so that everyone knows what you have
- A request to ask that people to share your post.

Of course, as with anything online, you want to be careful with whom you are sharing things, especially if you live alone. You might have reasons it would be inappropriate to post on Facebook or on Craig's List, for example.

I do not post my sales on Facebook – after all, there are some "friends" on Facebook, I wouldn't want showing up at my sale! Also, if your sale is a success – then you will not have much time to chit chat anyway!

BOXES and BAGS

Consider having boxes for customers to carry around with them – just think of yourself at a store, if you have 5 items and you're holding them close to your stomach so that they won't fall, you are less inclined to keep looking because keeping track of what's in your hands becomes a problem.

If you don't have boxes on hand for them to shop with, I like to keep an empty table by the checkout table, so that people can put their items on that table while they shop more. I also go up to them and ask them if I can take the items off their hands – so they are free to shop more! If you've worked in retail, you know how important this is!

If you have bags left over from all your couponing at the grocery store, Target, CVS, etc. be sure to save those and bring them out for your garage sale – it's nice to bag up a customer's purchases and hand over the items.

FRIENDS/FAMILY

Line up 1-3 people to help you out. Be sure that someone is the dedicated cashier. If your items aren't individually priced, be sure that your cashier has a price list with the color codes or tape the price list to the checkout table so it is easy to access.

SIGN UP SHEET

I print out a two column e-mail sign-up sheet.

When someone buys something, I say, "Do you enjoy going to garage sales? I have two garage sales a year and my mom and Aunt have one a year. If you want, you can give us your email address and we will contact you a few days before our next sale to give you get a heads up."

People are usually game. And furthermore – you have already confirmed that they are buyers that like your stuff. And if you know basic business principles, repeat buyers are your best customers.

As far as the sign-up sheet is concerned, one column has their name and one column has a space for their email. I also have a Sharpie marker that I put out with the sign-up sheet. I have found that when you give someone a big fat Sharpie they are more inclined to write legibly. Don't ask them to give you their email, ask them to write it down, so that it doesn't distract you from other buyers. Once they have written it down, I like to confirm that I can read their handwriting. After all, at the end of the day, I am the one that types that email address into a spreadsheet. Then the next time I have a garage sale I just copy and paste the addresses into the "BCC" field of the email announcement I'm going to send out.

	Garage Sale Email List	
	Lista para recibir una notificación de la venta en garaje	
	Sign up to receive a notification of next year's garage sale	
	Inscríbase para recibir una notificación de esta venta en garage para el año que viene	
	Name	**Email (Preferred)**
1		
2		
3		
4		
5		
6		
7		
8		
9		
10		
11		
12		
13		
14		
15		
16		
17		
18		
19		
20		

You'll see that we have the message in Spanish as well. We have many Spanish speaking patrons, so it's important to be bilingual (or have photos like those on the bulk signs to make the interpretation very easy). My mom and Aunt used to collect phone numbers before emails became popular. However, one year I made the phone calls to let people know about the garage sale. It was HORRIBLE. It took forever, people were confused about who I was and WHAT ON EARTH I was calling for. I do not recommend it!

Sometimes there are people who don't have email and want to give you their phone number – that's completely up to you if you want to call them. I just found it was not worth my time (or the headache).

CLEAN

Clean items sell best - so if your products have dust or anything like that on them, make sure to wipe them off - better chances of them selling that way.

CASH – CHANGE

Be sure to have a good amount of cash on hand so that if people need change, you have it.

Here's what to get in cash:

- $20 in ones
- $30 in fives
- $50 in tens
- $60 in twenties
- $10 in quarters (one roll)

CITY ORDINANCES

Check with your city if you need No Parking signs or for limitations on garage sales. My city requires me to "rent" No Parking signs – 5 of them for $1 each. And when I return the signs, I get my $5 back.

NO HESITATIONS!

Don't doubt that something will not sell in a garage sale! I have been amazed by the things that sell that I wouldn't pay 2 cents for! Stick it out on a table – what's the worst that can happen? It's doesn't sell and you donate it for a tax deduction?!

PRICING

Clear Pricing – One of the most annoying things about having a garage sale is being asked how much something is when you are trying to help five other customers. Be sure to mark everything – whether it's with a colored sticker that designates a price based on the color or if it's a numerical sticker that tells you the exact price – doesn't matter – as long as it's marked!

Before, after and During the Sale

People love to come to coupon stock pile sales because it saves them money without having to buy the products at the store for full price. People scan Craig's List for the next stockpile sale. It saves them time and money. Some people will buy your stock pile at a discount and will resell it at a flea market.

POST FLYERS

Be sure to post your flyers – hand them out to your neighbors, post them in your local hardware store or grocery store.

Be sure to check whether there are restrictions on placements of signs in your neighborhood and whether you need a permit to hold a garage sale.

PUT SIGNS OUT

You also want to put the signs that you made for the street out in strategic locations pointing back to your house. Again, you want to check with the city to see if they allow this.

ESSENTIAL ITEMS

Have a box ready that has all the stuff you need to price more items at the last minute (usually I forget to mark one or two things or have an idea at the last minute to make a sign) – so I keep the following things with me outside:

- Scissors
- Tape (scotch tape and mailing tape)

- Stickers for Prices
- Pen
- Paper
- Business Cards
- Calculator

LEAD GENERATION

Make the most out of your garage sale traffic for your home business or a charity run or whatever you might think help spread the word about an event/product that you support.

I have postcards out that people can pick up about Guide to Couponing.

DISCOUNTS

If you have your garage for 3 days – you might consider dropping everything to 50% off the last day or the 2nd to last day to help clear house!

When you set up for your sale, try to put like things together. If you sell from your stockpile, put all health and beauty items, food items, cleaning supplies, office/school supplies, etc. together.

When you have a slow spell or down time during your sale, walk around and straighten things back up – move them around, keep your tables looking neat. My mom and Aunt always joke about how when they straighten something up or move it around, it sells…and I'm not kidding – it always works. It's weird.

KIDS' TOY TABLE

If you have kids and are also having a traditional garage sale with your stockpile sale, then consider having a kid's area or a table where all the toys are so that the kiddos will be occupied while their moms or dads shop.

FOOD FOR FUEL

Having a garage sale requires a lot from your physically and mentally. Physically you will be on your feet all day and will be lifting and moving stuff around. Mentally – you're dealing with the public and whenever you're dealing with the public, there are different issues to deal with – not to mention the math you'll be doing that you're probably not used to doing all day long!

I am always exhausted after my sales and sleep well that night. However, it's important to fuel yourself with good quality snacks that are easy to eat if you're busy. Think power bars and apples.

BARGAINING

People will bargain. People will haggle. Be prepared. Think about what you're willing to take to get rid of stuff.

If someone is buying a lot of stuff and it totals $110 or something along those lines – I will tell them I will take $10 off or might throw in another shampoo or two. If I've been running the sale for 2 days, then I might take $30-$40 off. Just depends on the circumstances.

I usually do not bargain on the first day of the sale – unless, and this has happened, someone buys $400 worth of stuff – then I will take $50 off to get it out of there, so I can bring out more stuff. If someone asks me for a discount on 1-2 items, it just depends on what the discount is and if it's worth it. In general, though, I do not bargain on the first day of the sale.

LAST DAY OF THE SALE

I like to run my sales from Thursday to Saturday. Sometimes if I have a lot of product, I do it on Sunday too. But I usually find by Saturday evening I am exhausted and need Sunday to myself to recuperate. The last day of the sale you can make everything 1/2 off to move more stuff and then the last hours of the sale you can give everyone a grocery bag and tell them whatever they can fit inside is just $20 or whatever price you want to make it. Again, the goal is to make money and move stuff, so you don't have to move it back inside.

DONATE

I also like to have the donation person all lined up to pick up my stuff that Saturday afternoon or on Monday morning - so I can get my car back in the garage.

When your sale is done, find a local charity group that will pick up your Garage Sale leftovers – after all, Garage Sales aren't only for making money – but to get rid of stuff! Get it out the door for good by scheduling a pick up when it is over with.

Have Fun

I know, you might be thinking this is a ridiculous chapter – but it is so important. A garage sale can be stressful – but it doesn't need to be. People will probably steal. Let it go. Here's how I look at it – it's something that I wanted to get rid of anyway and if that person needed it so badly to steal it, then I hope I helped them. Or I resort to the notion of karma – they'll get what they have coming to them!

People can be a blast to talk to at garage sales. I have some people that will sit and talk to me for hours – which can be distracting when you're busy, but can be a welcomed gift when you're dead during certain hours.

This does bring up a good point which I will cover in the next chapter – safety.

But having fun is the most important step! You're making money and getting rid of stuff and cleaning up your stuff! Have fun in the relief!

Some of my favorite memories with my mom and my aunt are from our garage sales together – I have laughed so hard I have almost peed my pants or I have had to go inside so that I can control myself. You get some characters at garage sales and people asking the most random, weird things…and if they're asking your Aunt and you're eavesdropping, it can be pretty darn funny.

I have also had a good friend of mine run a garage sale with me and she was hilarious in the things that she would say to garage sale folks. It's funny how you can get so focused on the sale that you forget to have fun! So it's nice to have a friend around that keeps it fun.

Safety and Legal

BE SAFE

When you have a yard sale or a garage sale, you are exposing your home, your neighborhood, etc. Be smart.

Have at least one other person with you at the garage sale – never go it alone. I would suggest two more people if you have a bunch of stuff.

If, for some reason, I am left alone at my garage sale, I set my alarm – so that if I am put in a situation where someone demands to go into the house, the alarm will start going off when I enter or they enter.

Since you are making money from your sale – only keep around $100 in cash on you or on the cashier outside – put everything else inside and just take in chunks inside as you make it. That way, knock on wood, if you are ever robbed – they only get $100.

LEGAL?

Some people have legal concerns about having these types of sales. Of course, you need to first check with your city to see what the rules are as far as garage sales are concerned. There are often garage sale ordinances that exist in cities, especially smaller cities within bigger cities. But as far as I know, the couponing items - it's like anything else at a garage sale - you bought the product and now are getting rid of it because you don't want it anymore. They are your things now and you can do what you'd like with them.

Future Sales

Now that you know everything to expect, there are also ways to plan for future sales.

For example, to cut down on the pricing and organizing, I now price everything when I bring it home from the store. In other words, after every shopping haul that I bring home, I take it downstairs to my dryer – put everything on the dryer and then mark it for the garage sale (that is, I mark the stuff I know I am going to sell). And if you watch our YouTube channel https://www.youtube.com/guidetocouponing, then you also know I sometimes make a video while everything is laid out on my dryer and talk about my haul.

Keep your garage sale list up-to-date – take off any emails that are invalid and add any new people that might have signed up during your last sale.

Need money before your next sale? You might consider selling your items on Amazon, eBay or on Craig's List on an individual basis.

Online Resources

PLACE FREE ADS

- craigslist.org
- garagesalehunter.com
- yardsalesearch.com
- mytagsale.com

SELL ONLINE

- Amazon.com
- eBay.com

Garage Sale Sign Checklist

- Old political sign
- Scissors
- Clear packing tape
- Print outs from computer
- Stapler

Things to Do 3-4 Days before the Sale

- Post flyers at your kids' schools
- Post flyers in local stores
- Post flyers at your church
- Send out an email to friends and ask them to send it onto friends
- Get boxes from Costco - open boxes that have handles
- Make a list of specific brand items you have
- List your garage sale on Craig's List
- List garage sale on Facebook
- Get No Parking Signs or whatever your city requires for garage sale
- Get your street signs ready - the ones that point to your house
- Get your signs ready for the sale, ex. Cash Only, any other special signs like "Coke 50 cents"
- Send out an email to let people know garage sale is going on
- Make sure everything is priced or color coded
- Get Cash and smaller bills from the bank
- Do you have a business? For example, I put out postcards for my Guide to Couponing at my sales

Things to Do the Day of the Sale

- Put signs at the top and end of your street and on other major busy streets
- Put up No Parking Signs
- Take a photo of a table of your stuff - post it on your Facebook and invite people to come
- List your garage sale on Craig's List AGAIN
- Send out another email to friends and ask them to send it onto friends
- Put up your signs ready for the sale, ex. Cash Only, any other special signs like "Coke 50 cents"
- Put items out on tables – in like groups
- Put out flyers or anything else
- Have a positive attitude that you will sell, sell, sell!

Things to Do after the Sale

- Update your e-mail list of people that want to know about your coupon sales
- Put everything away
- Make notes of what sold well so you know what to stock up on
- Have a lot of left overs? Call a charity group and have them pick it up
- Have a lot of left overs? Put an ad on Craig's List offering to sell it altogether for $X amount. Put parameters on there like "must pick up and must pay cash".

Garage Sale Checklist

- Tables
- Calculator
- Cleaning Towel
- Pad of paper or clip board – if you have the sale with someone else you want a way to keep track of everything. Over 15 years ago, my brother got my mom a cash register for her birthday because of her annual garage sales – it has always come in handy.
- Cash Box/Fanny Pack – I prefer a fanny pack or a pocket where you keep the money in a wad on you.
- Cash - I usually have $20 in ones, $30 in fives, $50 in tens, $60 in twenties and $10 in quarters (or one roll). You won't want to miss a sale because you can't supply change! Once you've taken in some money, take out some of the larger bills and put it away in a safe place in the house.
- Stickers or Price Stickers
- Bags for shoppers
- Tape – Scotch and Mailing Tape
- Scissors
- Ziploc Baggies
- Signs
  - Garage Sale
  - Cash Only

- List on Craig's List

- Plastic bags or bubble wrap – to wrap breakable things when someone buys them.

- Fanny pack or carpenter's apron.

- Calculator.

- Card tables.

- Notebook and pen.

- Measuring tape.

- Garment rack.

- Full-length mirror.

- Extension cord. Allow shoppers to test lamps, radios, and other electrical appliances.

- Packing supplies. Have old newspapers, Bubble Wrap, plastic bags, and boxes on hand.

- Drink lots of water

Thank You for Reading *The Couponing Stockpile Garage Sale: A How To Guide*

A sincere thank you to you for reading *The Couponing Stockpile Garage Sale: A How To Guide*.

WHEW! That was a lot of information just for a 3-day garage sale, right? RIGHT! But! Believe me, it's like second nature now – if today's a Tuesday, I am now at a point where I could have a garage sale on Thursday. I am THAT organized now. So there is a way to make this a well-oiled machine to help you make the most out of your stock pile.

I hope that you will share your first couponing experience with us and your first stockpile garage sale on GuideToCouponing.com in days, months and years to come. You are always welcome to submit a story about your couponing stockpile garage sale journey to me through e-mail at info@guidetocouponing.com – if you want to share it on the site.

I would like to take this opportunity to say again that I spent a lot of time and effort creating this book and would appreciate it if you would respect my work by not sharing or distributing the book to anyone else without my permission.

If you have any suggestions, tips or criticisms of this book, please do not hesitate to contact me at info@guidetocouponing.com with any comments!

I am also always on the lookout for testimonials for *The Couponing Stockpile Garage Sale: A How To Guide*, if you are up for sending a testimonial, please think about the following questions:

- What kind of doubts did you have before starting to read this guide? Please be honest.
- How did the guide deliver on its promises?
- Who would you recommend this to and why?

While I do my very best to provide all the information that you need to have a couponing stockpile garage sale, I am only human and might have forgotten something.

Do you have any questions that I haven't addressed in this *The Couponing Stockpile Garage Sale: A How To Guide*? Please don't hesitate to ask me any questions by sending me an email to info@guidetocouponing.com I can make this book better if I understand what I might need to add.

New to couponing? You might want to first read our *Couponing for the Beginner: A Guide to Couponing for the Uninitiated*.

If you haven't already, I encourage you to subscribe to GuideToCouponing.com's newsletter, join us on Facebook, Pinterest, Twitter, Google+ and YouTube!

Thank you again for your purchase and I look forward to hearing about your great garage sale earnings!

©2013 Jenny Dean of GuideToCouponing.com

www.ingramcontent.com/pod-product-compliance
Lightning Source LLC
Chambersburg PA
CBHW040750200526

45159CB00025B/1833